CALM IN TROUBLED WATERS

By

Maureen Anne Browne

ISBN: 978-81-19654-92-5

First Edition: 2024
Rs. 200/-

Cyberwit.net
HIG 45 Kaushambi Kunj, Kalindipuram
Allahabad - 211011 (U.P.) India
http://www.cyberwit.net
Tel: +(91) 9415091004
E-mail: info@cyberwit.net

Printed at Repro India Limited.

Contents

BEYOND DIGITAL

The dawn has come,
but the sun hidden
by a sky empty, insipid,
dulling everything.

Gulls flood in,
their noisy speeches
irritating so much
I hardly notice their genius:

wide hinged wings
twisting, folding, curving,
to ribbon the sky, ride
the thermals, fly in circles.

As quick as a camera click
the sun brightening
my world with pictures
better than digital:

daisies open, denying
their fragility –
undisturbed by the breezes
blowing over them

disclosing the underside
of ivy, bending
the errant stems
in the tightly cut hedges;

shadows play
on the lawn,
gold leaf-curls fall,
downy feathers drift on;

old clematis,
faithful as ever,
adorning the side wall
with purple petals.

Things already seen,
but the sun brings
them to us
in such high definition,

igniting
that little spark in us
of just having
discovered something.

THE PROMISE

Inseparable,
sprawling up
the outside wall
of my house
clinging to white stone,
nothing to show
but bare bones
turned ashen,
interwoven like lattice.

Spring rousing the roots,
clothing the skeletons
with tendrils, leaves, shoots:
the ageing Clematis,
straggle-stemmed,
at the height of its powers
flaunting four bold magenta flowers,
the younger Wisteria
branching out with ease,
bringing the promise
of countless blossoms
in an avalanche of leaves.

If one of these,
so intimately bound,
must perish
so that one can survive
should I choose Clematis,
established,

blooming now,
or Wisteria settling,
full of potential?

Some say it is better
to travel hopefully –
however I decide,
cutting the ties
this close
I could lose both.

BRIAR ROSE

Young leaves
gathering
on the branches
camouflaging
the thorns.

Unseen energy
building
to silent explosions
of pastel pink roses,
hearts full, golden.

Petals breaking
from stem and stamen
to drift down
and soften stony places,
every bloom gone.

Berries cheering
the dull stems
with bright red
shells, full of goodness –
a salve for the unwell.

Beset by bitterness:
stems dead,
jagged-edged,
berries
wizened red.

I saw
the blood,
the thorn,
and knew
there'd be a resurrection dawn.

THE SIGNIFICANCE OF SMALL THINGS

You could easily pass me by
I am diminutive in size.
If the land is sea-swept or dry
I am adaptable and wise.

I am diminutive in size –
not weaker because I am small.
I am adaptable and wise,
I have dew if the rains don't fall.

Not weaker because I am small:
I have strength enough to survive
on dew where the rains don't fall,
and blending in helps me thrive.

I have strength enough to survive,
nourish myself with light,
I can blend in to help me thrive,
keep most of my leaves out of sight.

I nourish myself with light.
If the land is sea-swept or dry
I keep most my leaves out of sight.
You could easily pass me by.

THE BALLAD OF LIVING STONES

I lead an unconventional life
unseen, unsought, unfound,
I prosper in the wreckage where
the broken rocks abound.

Others stand as on parade
stark white against the green,
everyone is shown respect
it's such a solemn scene:

the furrows etched on every face
the timeless marks of pain
on the thousands who are standing up
for the thousands who were slain.

The blood-rich soil is at their feet
where sweet remembrance grows –
the tulip and the daffodil,
the heather and the rose.

I curve and blend to suit the world
and no-one stops for me,
then someone comes across the shale
and he stoops down to see

a thing he'd never seen before
in this dustbowl of a land –
he thinks I'm just a pebble till
he grasps me with his hand:

he finds I'm very much alive,
the squirrels pass me by,
I take a beating from the sun
and still refuse to die.

He apprehends my camouflage
with wonder in his eyes,
knows the joy of naming things
and carries off his prize.

I'm tended in a garden now,
I'm seen, I'm sought, I'm found;
men will climb a mountain
for me on my home ground.

GREEN TURTLE

The by-catch of your body
hangs in the net.

It wasn't always like this:

once, you floated
in the upper reaches of the ocean
on mats of sargassum,
swimming the tropical waters
foraging on reefs sprigged with coral,
diving for plankton;
muscles, lungs, growing stronger

for the long journey –

push your body,
with its scutes of olive and ochre,
through a thousand miles
of water till clear of the tide,
scoop out a nest with your flippers,
lay your eggs, take time
filling in, packing down,
a last flipperful of sand
for camouflage;

making the slow trek
back, to the surging
boulders of the deep, leaving
a slender hope on the beach.

THE SKY

The sun is seeping through the drifts
of endless smoky grey
until it cheats the night awhile
and gives us back our day.

It lets the gold of Autumn flaunt,
red-beaded hedges glow,
and man may work a few more hours
before he has to go.

And maybe you will get a chance,
or maybe even two,
to see the sky in swathes of pink
then bales of China Blue.

And when the Daystar leaves at last
and night is all above,
that vast abyss of black is filled
with candle-gems of Love.

BEARING IN MIND

My head, the summit
of myself, carries so much
around I wonder that there's
room enough in so small a size,

to hold the heights of Canada
on which a man can stand
and see, the same as Gulliver,
a land of tiny men;

fjords slicing Norway,
sheer-walled mountain sides,
boulders of frothy water crashing
through spruce and pine;

Arizona canyons
standing open-mouthed –
chasms of ancient granite
five thousand feet down;

monuments, cathedrals,
palaces, peoples;
memories keep increasing,
but never weigh me down.

My mind is an enigma,
and if a man is found
who *can* unravel the mystery,
then I will show him around.

HUMMINGBIRD

A fragile form
reflecting the essence of God
you come to the forest edge,
to Panyards and meadows
with the language
of love in your feathers –
ruby and emerald.

Open fans hinged
to your soft curved body
you mount the air
rising, dipping,
describing infinity;
hovering
to feed
with your needle beak
from the golden cups
of jewelweed,
pluck insects
from the silvered threads
of spiders' webs
till autumn starts
to draw out the dark.

Then you rise
and arc the sky
bridging a gulf
five hundred miles wide.

CLOSING TIME

After the exodus
the cobbles are obvious:
remnants of stress,
cigarette ends,
grouting the gaps,
strangers bedding down,
attached to each other,
anonymous bundles
on the Hohe Strasse.

The trains go on:

foreigners, locals,
white, brown, black, standing,
bags slung over shoulders,
laptops clasped,
lounging against handrails,
hanging onto straps,
sitting, passively accepting
the sandwich conditions,
wired to elsewhere looking
at nothing in particular,

or at fingers
stabbing mobiles,

getting on, getting off,
the only sounds
the hissing of doors,
the clatter of train on track.

Towering over
streets, trains, people,
the mediaeval features
of the great cathedral
still sharply defined,
still pointing upwards,
but for a while we retreat
into unconscious doing of things
– nobody speaks.

BEAUTIFUL OBSESSION

Become
the stars you see
on catwalk candy stalls
where fashion icons hang about
heaving,
screaming
through coats of gloss.

Tortured by images on front pages
run your fingers over polished faces,
catch the pinks and purples,
learn the sensuous secrets,
long for the same features:

sultry eyes,
hair that shines,
a luminous complexion,
limbs that are lithe.
No creepy lids, no sagging chin,
no bulges of fat on your thighs.

You cling
to whatever assurances they give
to make you the right shape
with the right skin
then, you will not be inferior to them.

You do what they advise:
use the right products,

diet, detox, exercise.
However hard you try
you never do
become the stars you see –
they lie.

ON THE EDGE

I sit on the edge
of my unmade bed
staring at pink wallpaper.

I should be singing
along with Celine Dion
as I lather my skin
with exotics from Africa;
dither over the slinky
blue dress with the split,
or the short black silk;
make up my face,
adding the glitter,
glam my nails.

The sun slips through
a chink in my curtains
dappling furniture,
glinting chrome and silver;
my mobile phone plays tunes
beneath the bedclothes;
mirrors can't seduce me;

I am down
the dark of my mind
feeling my way
through the rough,
the mistakes –
the taxi waits . . .

THE MAP OF MY MISTAKES

I read it daily,
manacled to guilt,
gripped
by the mirror's ability
to show up the insane
histories of my face:

indentations,
rough places,
discolorations –
the scars
of my own making.

Conscience failing
to dissuade me
I poke and prod
tiny volcanoes
till I draw blood,
loathe what I've done.

I look in the mirror
and imagine
a few deft strokes
of the brush,
the tactical choosing
of colours
and I will be attractive.

I go through my day
latching on

to shop windows,
chrome kettles,
mobile phones,
checking
the flaws are hidden.

Come evening,
I am alone
in my room
unmasked,
sinking myself
into the soothing
modulations of music,
drifting on beautiful words
till the brink of morning.

Tired of the hurt,
my head on the pillow,
mind scourged
with the words,
If only, if only . . .

The sun moves in
beaming,
as if by itself
could make me leave
these tangled sheets.

I stare at the ceiling.
The alarm-clock
badgering
I leave my bed,
look in the mirror
and imagine . . .

VIRGIN HAIR

A girl with no name curls
into a clutch of children cadging heat
under a manhole cover, sleeps

until hunger gnaws, returns
her to the street into air so bitter it is freezing
the Yinesi, wind hurling snow into heaps:

invisible to the fur-clad people
going about their business,
her pleas for help wasted breath,

she rummages in the rubbish dump
for a piece of potato, leavings on a bone,
a crust, but the dogs got there first,

hands red-raw, coat, ushanka, soaked,
feet too numb to tell her she needs new boots
hunger urges her on, to a door she knows

that says 200 roubles for virgin hair,
remembers her friend: dead,
stares and stares at the 200 roubles

and thinks, *O for a hot bowl of soup full
of carrot, cabbage, fish*, pulls off her hat,
a waterfall of thick auburn hair

tumbles down her back, she strokes it
a little, twists it round her finger,
whispers, Please mama don't be angry . . .

PAYING THE PRICE

A woman in her forties
sits on a balcony in California
eating oysters,

the sun sheening her tanned skin,
glinting her gold bangles,
her sapphire and diamond ring.

Fanning herself
with the latest edition of Upscale Living
kicks off her sandals,

peels back her linen blouse,
dons her Rayban sunglasses,
and settles down, into her rattan lounger.

Sipping a Chardonnay leans forward
to get a better look at couture on the sidewalk –
Dolce & Gabbanna, Gucci, Armani;

never-ending falls of hair –
provocative blonde, red, auburn, slithering
over bare backs, demolishing the myth

that a woman who is older
can never have hair like that – her mind races
to corn waves, chignons, French plaits:

pays out dollars by the hundreds
for virgin hair extensions,
real, Russian – no questions asked.

THE FUTILITY OF SELF

Our lives a tumultuous ride
of danger, success, failure –
we hold the rail of morality tight
to ensure our safety.

The better self lied –
however hard we try
to escape our nature the ride is fatal –
damned for our pride.

PROGRESS IN A FOREIGN LAND

Old Avarice he forced the hand
of Progress in a foreign land:
Progress, with the help of Pride,
would dam the river, control the tide.

With Impudence he worked in haste
and got a thousand folk displaced,
he gained the ground but he needed more
and stripped the trees from the forest floor.

Nature screamed when trees were felled,
she startled Earth when she rebelled,
when the dam had just been built
she blocked the reservoir with silt,

the ground beneath began to quake
for it had more than it could take.
The waters he'd walled would not be bound –
a town, a farm, a village, drowned.

Progress wasn't too distressed,
Ambition kept his mind obsessed
with all the things he could impound
if only he'd go underground.

When Power provoked him to be bold
he brought forth diamonds, silver, gold.
Progress in precocious mood
assumed the ground of Greater Good:

wooed the sceptics, spread the view
that global warming's nothing new.
Fumes from burning fossil fuel
grew more rampant, grew more cruel;

walls corroded, wildlife died,
cancer plagued the human side.
Progress wouldn't stay his hand,
he'd build the empire that he'd planned

till coral reefs are bled white,
and stars are driven out of night.

"THIS IS THE PLACE"

His sureness unstoppable
men followed him
through blizzards,
swarms of locusts, crickets,
drought, hunger, sickness,
till the hard ground broke,
and they were growing
potatoes, maize, oats,
raising their children
in settlements, villages, a city,
centred around the Temple

in a land blazing
orange and salmon:
higher thought written
with sandstone cliffs, fins,
buttes, bridges, pinnacles,
hills rich in jasper, topaz,
garnet, and a thousand
arches, doors standing open,
trusting you will not break
the delicate skin of the place
you have just come to

en-masse,
to climb the switchbacks,
cycle the appointed paths,
camp where it says you can,

stand where the famous words
were spoken, by another 'Moses',
learn its history, take photos,
return and return until
one day you come with a knife,
cut deep scars
into the side of Frome Arch.

CALM IN TROUBLED WATERS

Trees transformed
into flaming torches
blazing yellow, gold, orange,
rousing remembrance:

you came like a butterfly
moving through
harsh realities
soothing my soul.

I watch leaves
in strong colours losing
their connections,
falling in small flurries,

adrift like me
on a turbulent sea:
earth trembles,
monuments fall,

waters crashing
through their borders.
The dogs of war
savaging each other.

My wayward heart
would tend to fear
with the awesomeness
of it all, then I hear

you sweetly chide:
your quiet calm
won't let me run
away and hide.

In the autumn
of your life you came:
vibrant strength
within a fragile frame.

The lonely furrow
lonelier now you're gone;
I feel the gentle brush
of your wings – carry on

OASIS

In Colorado
anxiety rises
over too much snow –
avalanches likely;
disquiet in every state
over the man about to be
inaugurated.

In Northern Ireland
devolved government
has fallen,
public services
battling for survival,
words rattling
through cyber space,
accusation, denial;

the wind agitates
till the sea rises,
a leviathan freed
of its fetters thundering
towards us –
we place our hope
in sandbags at the door.

Outside the unease,
the disorder,
I am being absorbed
into a picture

of somewhere
I've never been –
the Karst mountains
of Southern China:

soft green hills,
rising, like pyramids,
from square
hedgeless fields
of emerald.
A dirt path
easy passage
into the distance,
the play of light
and sun and cloud
bringing me
into the mystic.

In spring
the emerald
turns to gold,
something I may never
witness, but knowing
it to be so
makes all the difference.

IN THE NURSING HOME

His battles were different now:
death coming at him
like a sloth bear – to maul;
his paratrooper's heart still strong.

Willing himself on:
reaching milestones –
across the room, into the hall,
inching down the long corridor,

holding on, to the rail, till
he makes it to the library, further,
further, till he reaches the lounge,
slumps into a chair to recover.

He'd tell me how far he'd got,
I'd feel so proud. One day he fell.
The power in his legs began to ebb,
his will still summoning itself up

to put one foot in front of the other,
for a shorter and shorter distance;
his will no longer able to override.
He said, I've had a good life.

WINTER

Not cold enough for the earth to glisten,
but bitter enough for the taking of things.

Your son keeps vigil, waits through the clock
ticking through the minutes until you slip from us.

Near the grave's edge men in black closing in
marking death. I clasp my cousin tight.
She's safe I said, I know she is. The tears still fell.

Her mother's eyes were always dancing,
like a sun-washed child's until, sight taken,
freed from the body that failed her.

After the burial the red flowers: carnation,
rose, helianthus, linger till they too are taken.

I remember her in blue, the gaiety in her eyes –
forget-me-not in the sunshine.

AFTERWARDS

Junk mail in the hall,
the phone on the floor
cut off.

I'm clearing,
wondering
how twenty years
of accumulations
could fit into
something this small.

Objects, separated
from their meanings,
waiting behind
glass doors
in the last cabinet
to be taken:
two red gold-rimmed
coffee cups
sitting on their saucers,
a pyramid of cut glass,
a Cornish pottery jug,
a marble lantern
with two doves;

they will move on,
sit somewhere else
for a while, re-loved,
or not.

The patch of dark
marking the spot where
the mahogany framed
picture was:
the field of bluebells
that became bluer
the closer you drew.

A skip will be waiting
outside the door
for the kitchen cupboards,
the Belfast sink,
the vinyl floor.

Freed from
the weight of things
this room fills up
with light, the sun
playing in new places:
corners, walls, indentations.

TIME-THIEF

He came at my beginning
a shadow I didn't see,
for years now oblivious
that he was pilfering me:

by small degrees of clarity,
the brittling of the bone –
sight, sound, mobility,
all are overthrown;

took the last breath from me,
thought my day was done;
he'd only freed my tethered soul,
I rose to meet the Sun.

FINDING YOUR PLACE

Everything foreign:
a babble of sounds,
fuzzy colours,
the feel of cotton;

on auto for a while,
rooting and sucking;
learning how to turn
want into cries;

the toil of teetering
until you stand,
of naming things –
yacht, ball, bat;

widening the path
of your wandering
till you pitch your tent
like your tribe;

settle into roles
and rhythms,
balancing work and leisure,
raising children;

energy flagging,
age in the bone,
almost filling
the circle given;

restless, resigned,
the rust of time
taking you down,
to dust.

CONSIDERING THE DEAD

We pay so much attention to the dead:
making sure they are lovingly washed
and well dressed, ensuring their longevity,
lessening the look, with chemicals.

Place them in solid oak coffins,
three layers thick, to be swathed
in swansdown covered with satin,
six brass handles on the outside to carry them;

give them an extra set of clothes,
along with things they can use –
a hammer, a candle, a watch and chain,
and four handkerchiefs, perhaps a rose;

we let them rest awhile in amber glow,
keep watch for a time until
the lid is closed, adorned with a blaze of lilies,
and they go into the dark alone.

Some things break down,
others go on adding to their own kind
already there, hindering
the earthworm's ability to bring light, air.

SET IN STONE

Strange,
how a kind of permanence sets in
from things precarious:
waters rising, falling;
salt beds drifting; winds carousing,
lifting, shifting
to forge rock
that looks a full sun in the face,
and into the eye of a hurricane
with the same equanimity and grace.

But you are different:
needing rest and shade
you gouge out a home,
gather your blankets,
a battered saucepan,
makeshift knives and axes
around you and stay on.

So much you didn't know,
but you learn:
how to trap beaver,
the right places
to gather the berries,
dealing with the unstable seasons,
clearing your path as you go
till you feel less easy
with the sun, somehow,
and the cold.

That hardiness
with which you met the wild
deserting you now,
but you had come too far
to simply die.

You turn
to this unflinching mass of stone:
with your hand,
and its tremor you can't control,
scratch out your history with a blade
so that those, the curious,
the ones who simply stumble
upon it, will know
from this enduring page
that you existed,
came, and stayed.

MONUMENT

You took the blows: a tyrant, wanting you,
cut you out of your home, left you, to lie low
until he'd tightened his hold on lebensraum. O,
he'd raise you grand, but never followed through –
he dreamed too big of things he couldn't do,
and you confirm what all mankind should know,
were hammered, chipped, chiselled to show
what hatred, on the unbridled tongue, came to –
unspeakable bloodguilt, that stains us all.
Yet, on this broad reach of darkness, a light:
Jewish courage shone for the last fight.
You became a message forged on the sacred wall:
guard the tongue, and each man's right to be –
that is not down to you, it is down to me.

THE ANGEL OF THE NORTH

Hope:
rust-coloured
corten colossus,
narrow-ribbed
skittle body,
panelled wings
outstretched
in welcome
you hold
the threadbare hill,

crowning
the achievements
of past workers
bent double
underneath it
fighting the earth,
with pick and shovel,
for the black gold,
needed to keep the fires
going in industry, home.

You fostered
fondness in the young:
for one small boy,
rooted in the same soil,
it was love –
he signed his name
thinking thousands come,

go, they'll remember
my name on the Angel;
officials erased it.

You came
in pieces
to a run-down town
twenty years ago:
rose to become
a masterpiece,
a curiosity,
provocative,
some welcomed you,
some did not.

FLORENCE NIGHTINGALE'S APRON

Crisp white
full-front shield,
tied tight against
rustling skirts,
coming face to face
with long rows
of disease-ridden soldiers,
to take the filth:
spattered with
the spit of curse,
smeared with mud,
gunpowder,
wiped by hands
that bathed the blood
from gun-shot wounds,
gashes made
by sword,
bayonet,
contaminated
with cholera,
dysentery,
felt the bristled face
nudging in, caught
by a trembling hand,
became a map
written with man's need,
man's smudge,
man's smell –
I'd have to burn
to be clean again.

THE VICAR OF HUTTON ROOF

A man who loved the country ways
he'd walk among the Fells,
have summer nights upon the cragg
with glow-worms weaving spells.

His home was in a splendid place
where every view would please:
the rolling hills of Cumbria
with beech and chestnut trees.

The gentle folk of Hutton Roof
would find an open door:
a tramp was given a decent meal
and often he got more.

With courtesies well-honoured here
the pace of life was slow,
but men were dying out in France,
he knew he had to go.

A slight and ageing country man,
with eyes that often failed,
he tried to join up many times
but younger men prevailed.

This self-effacing saint of God
determined to be heard:
insisted he was fit enough –
they took him at his word:

conferred on him a Captain's rank,
as Chaplain he's fourth class,
his uniform and Maltese Cross,
his all-important Pass.

Etaples had a haunted look
with thousands passing through
like animals for slaughtering,
and little he could do.

He knew his place was at the Front
and won the right to go
as Padre to the Lincolnshires,
and these he'd get to know.

A service was of little use,
from thousands he'd get ten.
He found a better way than that –
go through it with the men.

To trenches that were troughs of sludge
with walls of ice and snow,
and frost enough to kill a man
the Padre chose to go.

He hauled his body through the mire:
to every post he'd come
with fresh supplies and cigarettes
and time to read to some.

It wasn't just a now and then,
but every night for sure
and every battle they were in
the Padre would endure.

He'd dress their wounds and talk to them,
distract them from the pain
and the shells still screeching round them,
the never-ending rain.

For every soldier that had died
the proper thing was done:
through hails of fire he said 'the words'
and stood for every one.

They've roses now in Hutton Roof:
here everything is black
except for poppies in the mud,
but there's no turning back.

The fighting got much fiercer still
for Passchendaele was worse
and tons of mud were sliding down
like some satanic curse.

All night he pulled them from the swamp:
for every friend he'd fight,
there was no letting up on this,
for them he'd do it right.

He praised the deeds of other men
and shied away from fame.
It was with great unease he wore
the medals when they came.

The bishop tried to keep him safe
by urging him to come
to Caldbeck in a country shire
and for a princely sum.

The Padre hoped he'd not offend,
but felt constrained to say
the Front was where he ought to be
and that's where he would stay.

Before the Germans sued for peace
their gunners still had fight:
the Padre's friends were raked with fire
and cut down in his sight.

As always, he looked after them:
his quiet loving style
transcending all the ugliness,
his reassuring smile.

They're on the fringe of winter now
and plans were going well:
his friends had taken up their place
along the river Selle.

He joined them for a little while
to chat, or just be near,
and then when he was going back
a shot rang out so clear.

They'd never see his face again –
that cheeky childlike grin.
The Padre whom they loved was dead –
they couldn't take it in.

No longer would he come to them
through mist or snow or rain
to calm them when they shook with fear,
to palliate their pain.

The young lads and the hardened men
felt utterly bereft:
he’d been so much a part of them
an awful void was left.

He came with unconditional love
and ‘woodbines’ in his pack,
went through the fires of hell with them
and never once turned back.

EVIL UNDER THE SUN

Who will speak up
for the Chinese people of Nanking city,
acknowledge their suffering
at the hands of Japanese soldiers
perverting the way of Bushido,

who will speak up
for the babies they bayonetted,
the children, the maidens,
the old women, they raped,
the civilians they decapitated,
the prisoners they injected
with cholera, mutilated –
stomachs ripped open,
limbs frozen, amputated?

History recording, debating, statistics.
Each one of the countless victims
had a name when living.

Who will speak up
for the Chinese people of Nanking city?

Will Purple Gold Mountain, there
when they were being burned to death
their bodies thrashing writhing
their screams hammering the air,
or the tons of earth
they were buried alive under,

or the Yangtze River
that caught them when they fell,
blasted with bullets, turning it red?

Who will speak up
for the Chinese people of Nanking city?

Who will remember
the acts of kindness from their own,
those of another country,
American, Danish, German,
driven by a common humanity
to do something?
The Pastor, the Missionary,
the Teacher, the Nazi, stood between,
saved thousands of Chinese.

We must speak up
for the Chinese of Nanking,
we must remember
those who came with compassion,
defied the danger, and took them in.

'. . .THE BEAUTY THAT STILL REMAINS.'

(*The Diary of a Young Girl*)

Here,

a place too far from anywhere,
the sun is precious:
no chrome or lavish patinas,
no white cups clean-gleaming,

no mirrors to verify his condition:
he reads himself
in the faces of others, and knows
the truth of his disfigurement.

Clad only in cotton, standing
on the hard ground of Siberian winter,
Red Guards pounding him with, Reform
through labour! Reform through labour!

Filling his clothes no longer, his mind
clinging to the silk lines of the Bible
and Chinese poetry. He sees the sun no less
beautiful, the river he has freed sparkle.

HOME

Not the nurturing kind:

a Chinese child
in my own country,
no mother,
racked with hunger,
seeing blood over and over,
Japanese soldiers
wielding bayonets

killing us daily –
mothers, fathers,
children, babies,
and the blood runs
on through the rivers,
the streets,
the blood of the Chinese:

I fled

to where a boy
could be
just anything he wanted,
or so they said.
I drank the streams
of freedom free, plucked
the fruit of a thousand trees:

went to school, found
Shakespeare, jazz, film,
majored in English,
dreamed big –
an American guy,
partial to hamburgers,
barbecue ribs, apple pie.

Like a young shoot, grafted
to another tree, nourished
by its root I grew,
differently from me –
home needled, comfort
unsettling my soul, bridging
the gap, fetching me home . . .

THE RETURN

I came home
with a heart full of hope,
and a cargo of light:
books, to give them
knowledge,
help them grow,
music, to elevate their soul,
dreams to hold.

My people weak
from hunger,
minds shuttered,
by a Way that allows
no other –
my hope muzzled:

American ways
spurned,
great minds
smothered,
friends turned
into people
I didn't know:

it cost my freedom,
my strength,
nevertheless,
someone else
would come,
open the shutters,
let in the sun.

LAOGAI

Chinese Labour Camp

Through the hours of standing, sitting,

I see you in your khaki tunic,
proud to be an Iron Girl
working for the revolution.

That night in Shanghai we were caught
in the tide: lanterns, dragons; children,
adults, singing songs of Mao.

Those moments in the field
of primroses: I held you close
my little moon, dared to kiss you.

*

Today, with dozens of others,
I was walking in circles 'outside':
a small room with a gaping hole in the roof.

We try to survive on toad, lice, rat.
Tonight, we will lie on the floor like
Mahjong tiles – tight-packed.

In our grey and white stripes,
patches of blanket sewn together for jackets,
swollen faces, skin infected, purple fingernails

we are in ruins, the famine taking over.
Come soon, my darling, I need to know
if I am human.

ON THE FACE OF IT

You lead the world
in digital technology,
commerce thriving
in your sprawling cities
with gleaming high-rises,
sleek fast trains riding the rails
for thousands of kilometres
connecting the provinces.

You take your place
at the round table,
with other nations,
helping to address
the pressing cases:
human rights,
climate change,
making the world safer.

Xinjiang
gets more police stations,
high-tech surveillance
to monitor the Uyghurs,
colleges for vocational training,
re-education – high walls
barbed, solid black gates,
watchtowers.

From his high pillar
Mao Zedong's

sculpted figure
haunts this place,
feet astride,
right hand raised.

Out of sight,
behind the black gates,
the tiger chair,
the electric batons,
the shackles,
men crying in the night.

THE BEAUTIFUL HOUR

Guns thunder,
fires rage in the rubble,
people flee in hundreds,
air chokes on smoke, debris,

love, works its wonder:

heavy bombing
reaching Moshchun
blitzing to pieces,
reaching Kyiv her home city –

she puts on her white blouse,
long sleeves embroidered
with red roses wreathed in leaves,
crimson plakta, black bodice,

fingers tremble putting on
her coral pink beads,
floral tiara: red, turquoise,
green, matching ribbons stream.

He puts on his white vishivanka,
grey stand-up collar and front panel
patterned with white line diamonds,
beige trousers.

Fresh faces oozing innocence,
hearts racing, hand in hand they run

into the danger, shells pounding
homes, cathedral, installations,

she pulls on him to stop, stares
at the slumped body on the street,
can't look at his face, can't not –
his eyes defiant, hers awash with tears,

he nods, draws her near,
they run on, past charred mangled cars,
until they reach it, take the steps down,
down into the sacred:

enfolded in scenes of holiness,
each holding a lit tall-stemmed candle,
they kneel at a small mahogany altar
to seal their love for each other.

The Pastor, black beard, glasses,
in shimmering silver damask,
solemn, gentle, moved by a love
so tender, sees them through the ceremony.

The beautiful hour over they change
into the fawn and green of a soldier,
smother each other with kisses, retrieve
their semi-automatics and leave – separate , , ,

SEPARATION

A teddy,
knit in garter stitch,
dark brown,
red-nosed,
dangling unscathed
in a tree of charred bones.

How did it come to be
caught in a tree
like a para missing the field?

What of the child,

who cuddled into it
when the bangs came
too loud and felt
safe for awhile?

Is the child trapped
under the hot heaps
of glass, metal, concrete;

curled into basement dark
with a dozen others
trying to learn the three R's;

lying in a hospital theatre,
doctors, tears in their eyes,
trying to save her?

Where is the child?

The blackened husks
of war growing blacker
with evening,
rain, sun, weaving
the colours –
a rainbow comes.

THE TALL MAGICIAN

London street children were recruited for the Empire

London sitting
like ships in a fog,
ragged children,
bare feet, torn britches,
upturned dirty faces,
we latch on
to the look and voice
of the tall man all in black:
high hard hat,
coat down to the cobbles,
baggy sleeves that dance
to the quick movements
of his hands.

What does he mean the tall magician

about planting children,
wanting an English child
like me to go with him
across the biggest sea
in the world, to where
the vines are laden
with the juiciest grapes
you've ever tasted,
pulling a big black bunch
from his sleeve,
and there's red and green,

dozens of them
trailing over the trellises,
trees tumbling
with things I'd never seen,
that I could eat –
pineapple mango lime
apricot pear peach
that go on for miles,
and all within reach,

what does he mean the tall magician?

I can't keep my eyes open,
but what does he mean?
I just want somewhere
to sleep. He is leaving,
his long coat swishing
in the breeze, I remembered
those trees, "Wait for me".

WAITING

She looked and looked the road he'd come,
her looking was in vain
like the waiting of the dried-out earth,
for the coming of the rain.

The land was spent and her son had left
for a city far away,
there'd be a job with a better life
and he'd send her half his pay.

The days went on and on and on
and not a word sent he,
she turned to heaven and begged for help,
O bring my son to me!

She could not settle to her tasks
the way she used to do,
with a merry heart and a twinkling eye,
for the city filtered through

in frenzied whispers of those who came
wearing their shiny shoes,
to tell of white men gambling
with hundreds of rands to lose;

a white boy had been murdered,
the streets were full of fight,
they're going to hang a black boy –
don't matter if it's right.

She grips her chest and cries to heaven,
What monster can it be
that plants such evil in the young,
O bring my son to me!

With hope as thin as a gossamer wing,
she'd clear and plough and sow,
but her mind and heart were on the road
as only a mother can know.

The clouds were gathering above her head,
and thunder cloyed the air,
heaven emptied its cargo of rain,
but she wept for the son not there.

THE RAINBOW

He works his boat saying nothing:

rain drizzling,
Copelands barely visible,
everyone soaked.

The children,
tiny fishermen,
all arms and shoulders
and rustling coats, shuffle in
to the edge of the boat,
with man-sized seriousness,

knuckles white
holding the rod tight,
but not too tight,
eyes full of purpose
keeping the line steady,
staring down into the murk.

The others
were reeling mackerel in,
boasting numbers,
why weren't they coming to him?
suddenly, the tug, rod bouncing,
he's screaming "got one got one",
turning and turning the handle,
losing his balance,
a hand more knowing

goes over his and he gets it in
the slithering fish:
shimmering skin,
pink and gold and silver tinged,
the sad button eye looking
up at him. He slips the hook
from where he made the wound,
casts the creature back.

The others laughed –
he'd nothing to take home.

Hiding his tears
he watched them
leave the harbour,
their animated figures
going farther and farther,
could still hear their laughter,
trying hard to believe
it didn't matter.

ALBATROSS

Feeling a sense of being less,
having no child, I walk
in shadow most of the time –

unable to face

family occasions:
sons and daughters paraded,
bragged about at the table;

travelling – a mum on the train,
toddler in a buggy, the other one
turning isles into runways;

the afternoon full of children –
chit-chatting, piling into cars, running
into outstretched arms.

I pull back, like a turtle
into its shell, too deep for even
my husband's love to reach.

The sea goes on

washing the rocks over and over,
whispering to the beaches as though
they were worthy of secrets,

I am here with my hurt,
though it were deep as hell . . .

MEMORY TREE

Dad,

I remember how you'd carry me around,
show me the tree you were growing
and say that it was ours.

We watched the dream unfolding:

the silver, then the green,
the rosy buds, enveloping nectar,
waiting to open their snow-white centres
to become baby apples.

I loved the perfumed petals,
the tiny anthers powdered yellow.

The blossoms went – it felt like a death,
nevertheless, the leaves kept on sugaring,
sheltering, strengthening.

"Look look," you said pointing,
and whisking me into the air –
"Pick one, we'll share."

Our teeth dug in: small bites big bites
tearing through the skin, champing
down to the core, giggling
as the juice ran down our chin,

as the clouds burst and we rushed
for the door, the door you walked
out of when you chose to see me no more –

What did I do wrong?
I was ten, cried and cried as if you were dead,

our tree gone.

GHOSTS

A child
urgent with living keeps
the hurt that seals a fear
in her mind at a distance

All her life
it lies a latent
volcano murmuring
unnerving

His drinking
his fists drove
her to wish she could
unexist him

A country
then a couple of towns
now a few suburban miles
all that's between them

The ground
slipping from under her
she tries smothering
her fear with busyness

Older reflective
ghosts who are not
benign gathering
momentum mocking

time – it doesn't
break their power
letting go
that is hard

TOO LATE

My mother kneeling in the dirt
looking around for someone
to be there for her haunts my mind.

We were young, caught up
in the red sun rising, devoured
words till they spilled over our tongue

in mantras that hurt love: friends, family,
the enemy if they did not succumb
to the cult of our Benevolent Father.

Good cadres full of fervour,
we 'struggled against' our teachers:
foul-mouthed, beat them;

my mother would not bow
to such a self-obsessed creature, said
the purged leaders should be returned.

I told her to retract her words:
she tore down his image,
then burned it.

I turned into something other,
scourged her with words
too cruel to tell,

handed her over knowing
what it meant. Outside the city
someone else pulled the trigger.

Now, my tears begging
forgiveness, I lay a trail of pink
and yellow petunias on her grave –

I am kneeling in the same dirt,
my face lowered to the earth,
aching to take back my words.

EATING MY WORDS

The common currency
of words is everybody's
business. By invitation,
or unbidden, I worry
them for hours. Commit
them to paper, wear down
my pencil lead trying to say,
in a new way,
what's already said,

changing, re-arranging
each word until it earns
its place in villanelle, sonnet,
ballad, kyrielle, free verse,

give them punctuation:
colons, commas, full stops.
An aid to understanding,
or just cluttering the place up?
The words that fail, litter
the reams of paper, must
be got rid of or else linger:

cross-shredded, dumped
in the brown bin to lie with
withered chrysanthemums,
fish bones, onion skins.
Returned to the earth
to be eaten by worms,

to nourish roots,
encourage a blade of grass,
a leaf, a tree –
perhaps.

IN THE MARKETPLACE OF WORDS

I scan the shelves:
row upon row of books
presenting themselves
in coloured jackets.

Up close I feel their spines,
see names, titles, a photograph.
Under lights, in the shade –
all waiting
for someone to engage.

I pass over
the illustrious: Arnold, Yeats,
Tennyson, Rimbaud,
the lesser known: Aiken,
Dowson, Bogan, Drayton,

dip in and out
of linen-coloured pages,
read the recommendations –
'A tremendously good book',
'A treasure trove',

drawn to a slim volume:
I prise you out,
a woman – enticing
me into your light
the others subside,

I am seduced
by unshakeable strength,
by a joy that survives –
black, beautiful, still you rise.

THE LAST SLAVE

Ah, Milton, you had the edge:
born free, white, for half your life
able to see the sun-dappled days highlighting
Copper Beech, Columbine, Meadowsweet,

the slow movement of clouds meeting,
parting, dulling and brightening the hours,
the dazzling tribes of the night sky –
Alpha Persei, Seven Sisters, Gemini,

a scholar of the finest college, fluent in Italian,
wrote, in English and Latin, papers on policy, theology,
poems, tracts, impacting Kings and commoners,
your legacy the touchstone of poetic craft.

*

Wiggins, born black, a blind autistic slave all his days,
unschooled, yet found his way, through sound:
a child entranced by music, played back pieces,
heard from children, on piano with precision,

grew up listening to tunes whistled by the wind,
staccato rhythms of rain on corrugated tin,
dramatic drumrolls of thunder, the beat of a swan's wing,
yodelling coyotes, the rich-toned songs of orioles;

delighting in domestic din – pot lids rattling
on a busy stove, water gushing from a faucet,
batter beaten, milk sloshed, chairs dragged

across the floor, the tic tock tic of the clock.

Bringing wonders from the piano, his own compositions,
he endeared himself to thousands of Americans
up to the President – used well the talent given.

THINKING BACK

The room remained
forbidden.

We kept our distance
busy being children:
learning to write
with chalk and blackboard;
baring our feet
to the warm tarmac;
teetering on walls.

Some things
escaped being hidden:

a Swastika,
part of the jumble
in our living-room cupboard;
a photo,
faded sepia,
of you in army uniform;
the Condor tin
preserving your medals:
a brass one, bigger
than an old penny,
a yacht on its face,
coloured bars, your wings.

The further I get
from these tokens of war

the more I return.
One thing gnaws:
that room –
was it your way
of protecting us,
or a covering up
of what you wished
you hadn't done?

OPEN HOUSE

A fire burned
that never went out.
Round about were doors:
six of them open

to cleaning; butter churning;
baking cakes and wheatens;
embroidering; reading;
arriving and leaving –

farmers, the Post Mistress,
those in service, labourers,
clergymen, the blacksmith,
the village schoolmaster:

rooms animated chatter
from people gathered around
the turf that gave them heat
and aromatics.

The seventh door
was into the dark – shut,
sealing in secrets; no-one
went in, no-one came out.

I stared, stared
half-wanting to try
the lock, stared at the brown
wood until I saw the cross;
remembered,
I only had to knock.

OVER THERE

A shadow,
too far away
to spoil
haymaking,
blackberry-picking,
cricket at the corner,
afternoon tea.

Rosy-coloured evenings
around the green
chenille covered table
bearing our magic lantern:
a pink-tinted globe
with clear glass chimney
feeding us light
from a pool of paraffin –
conjuring cosiness.

Unheeding of boundaries
houses crowd the fields
once ploughed for barley,
the mountain views
are smaller,
the cobbled farmyard
swallowed.

The house in shadow:
the beautiful orange wood
piano – its own

little brass candlesticks –
an ornament holder.
Standing in the corner
a small television
thunders with the sound
of guns and horses.
An old woman leans
into the black and white
fuzziness mesmerised
by 'The Lone Ranger'.

CHANGE IS A GIVEN NOT OPEN TO DEBATE

Change is a given not open to debate,
we should not hold too tightly onto things,
man is not the master of his fate.

We dig in, build, accumulate,
our security success with all the trimmings.
Change is a given not open to debate.

Everything we have acquired to date
will be taken from us. For all his strivings
man is not the master of his fate.

Hold lightly. Take time to appreciate
the beauty a single dewdrop in the sun brings.
Change is a given not open to debate.

New beginnings are reasons to celebrate,
because the dawn has come the blackbird sings.
Man is not the master of his fate.

Unknown or numbered among the great
feed the soul with nature's blessings:
change is a given not open to debate,
man is not the master of his fate.

BELFAST SUMMER

She looks out:
wind shifting the bins,
tossing litter into drains,
rain splattering the windows,
puddling the lanes,
with a curt *typical* returns
to her case full of summer:

she loves the look and feel of them –

the floatiness of orange chiffon
kissing her skin with silkiness,
frilly bikinis in aquamarine,
pink candy, lemon sizzle,
crisp cottons, quirky bottles crammed
with passion fruit, jasmine, apple-blossom,
strokes the diamonds on her strappy sandals
and imagines: palm trees lining the streets
and promenades of sun-soaked Alicante;
curling her toes in the warm sand
and drinking pina coladas;
a blue-green ocean swishing like petticoats,
its frothy edges flirting with sea urchins.

Places the last two pieces, straw hat, suntan lotion,
takes everything out, puts everything in, shuts the lid.

Takes note of the clock,
picks up her suitcase and sets off:

joins the human seas streaming
into lounges, Costa cafés, duty-frees,
sits down to relieve her feet
from ridiculous heels.

Neon lights flicker on one-armed bandits,
kids clank their handles,
a small girl throwing a tantrum,
she can't wait for Alicante.

A rush for the monitors,
gasps of astonishment, clamouring
for answers, clambering over baggage,
the Tannoy adamant no-one will get going:
an ash cloud over Iceland is changing
the chemistry of the heavens.

She watches rivers of rain revelling on the windows.

Turns to her leopard skin suitcase,
yanks it in front of her, trails it back
into the Belfast summer cursing the puddles.

STRANGE TIMES

Dragging
my body
from sleepless night
through morning,
afternoon, evening,
trying to fight
these feelings:

edgy
in crowds –
parks,
towns,
stations,
shopping centres,
theatres,

fearing
the three-sided mirror –
blatant,
You must lose weight,

dreading
the fluorescent
showing up
my imperfections.

Covid comes

aggressive:
shutting the door
on business, leisure,
forcing orders
from the top,
Stay at home –
Save lives,
Protect the NHS.

So much time lost:

nevertheless,
the world stopped,
I was able to jump off.

TAKING THE STRAIN

Struggling to deal with

a dangerous unseen
that's crossing borders
with the ease of water,
and lethal as weaponry,

seeing the long line
of coffined bodies
waiting
in the makeshift cemetery,

keeping our distance:
no gathering at weddings
or christenings, no being there
for the dying,

people idling
on streets, beaches,
asserting their freedoms,
energizing the enemy,

we are in jeopardy.

PATCHWORK QUILT

Confined to our own patch
by something insidious
that is killing us,
rending asunder the seams
of our Comforter:

threads, joining together
family, friends, severed;
losing the warmth
of tenderness –
the language of love
in kisses, hugs,
the catchups in coffee shops;
losing the cheerful colours –
parties, dancing,
the air sizzling
with banter;
losing that snug feeling –
in a mass of fans
deliriously shouting
support from the stands.

Fabric cut-offs
too small to be made much of.

WE CAN STILL SING

Our wings clipped
by some infectious
deadly invisible,
phone lines fizzing
with what when how if . . .
broken promises
littering every continent.

Shocked

into confronting
ourselves in the raw,
as if the Creator
of the cosmos
saw we were
already floundering
and pressed pause;

shocked

into considering
others – listening,
talking, compensating
for what was lost
parcelling out our children;

shocked

into finding joy

in noticing the parochial –
how the bloom
on a Rhododendron
comes like an acorn
in a six-point star of dark,
how the petals
of the pendulous Wisteria
resemble a Lupin,
but daintier,
how the Forest Flame burns
slow, dull, unable
to live up to its name,
until patience turns it to blazing.

THE COMING

Census day brought rivers of colour:
red turbans, black skull caps, long and short
tunics in yellow, purple, with leather girdles,
thonged sandals; dialects, languages, merging,
diverging down every street in Bethlehem.

Muleteers and herdsmen jeering, jostling,
trying to find bedding, fodder, women
carrying jars of water, landlords arguing,
striking bargains, the clatter of armour
as soldiers goaded people into order.

Bartering for cloth, wine, olives, went on
till the sky was strewn with stars, lamps
burning, small suns brightening the dark
of rooms and stables, air hung over with
liquor, sweat, dung, the town settling.

In the fields shepherds tightened their coats.
In a simple home – white stone,
earthen floor, nestling, with all the others,
into the hills, a boy was born, wrapped
in cloths and laid in a feeding trough.

Had they known who it was broke
into their world that day would they have left
their weaver's loom, their market stall,
stopped their potter's wheel, their raucous talk,
to seek a stranger out and kneel.

INDIFFERENCE

The prophets told it long ago,
the stars in heaven too
and even when it happened,
and when it all came true,
the world went on unheeding
it had other things to do:
like the jeering and the jostling,
the swearing in the night,
the bargaining with landlords,
with the mean and with the tight,
for the drink it did the talking
in the bargaining for rooms,
yet here, a cold and vulgar place,
the rose of Sharon, perfect love, blooms.

The Advent season has begun,
the preacher once again
is in his pulpit preaching
how God has come to men.
Only a handful of listeners,
most are passing the door
to join the countless others
in the buying more and more,
parties dizzy with sparkle,
downing drinks for fun,
a kind of compensation for those
who are bruised and broken
from trying to measure up,
do what can't be done.

DENOMINATION

The seaside church
could boast a choir fifty strong,
contraltos, sopranos, basses, altos –
notes blending into fragrant song.

All are gone – the church unused,
untended, moths merrily munching through
yards of presbyterian blue, mice scratch
and scuttle about desecrating the organ pipes.

The city church
in fine form on the outside: mighty pillars,
stout walls, dullness revived
with soft cream that gladdens the eye.

Inside everything gone: pulpit, pews,
communion table, font, replaced
with safes, counters, jingling of silver,
thumbing through notes with a rubber thimble.

CHRISTMAS MARKET

Tonight, the drab tones
of Belfast have turned to gold:

lights blazing
on pine trees,
the carousel,
the edges of the Ferris Wheel,
the little eaves
on cabins in blue, green,

attracting people
of all ages to buy

from stalls drowning
in shiny decorations,
wooden I-phone cases,
leather-worked bracelets,
crystals, wish bags, angels,
antiques, paintings;

dine on food
from distant places –
German schnitzel,
bratwurst, strudel,
Greek kebabs, halloumi fries,
Chinese noodles;

flood into pop-up pubs
for amaretto,

mulled wine,
prosecco,
or into the Gin Tin
for a tipple

to the background music
of the Salvation Army playing hymns.

CHRISTMAS EVE

Outside in the night,
gravitating to soup centres
and subways, the lonely,
the homeless, the hungry.

The clock strikes twelve,
the church is warm:

all well-fed and gathered in,
on blue cushions in polished
pews, to remember
the Babe of Bethlehem:

Divinity wrapped small,
Eternal God born
in a place open to all –
the poor, the broken, the lost;

some say it was a stable:
the cattle, the fodder, the filth;
others a poor man's dwelling,
the donkey brought in at night.

Either way we sing,
and over hills and towns and villages
a thousand bells ring,
for God is with us.

REFLECTION

The church empties,
with a merry Christmas
the canon shakes the hand
of his last parishioner,
stands, eyes wide
on the night sky:

a heavenful of stars
to wonder at
he forgets, for a while,
congregation dwindling,
lack of young people,
choir missing;

the stars, witness
to the first Christmas,
cheer his desponding heart –
they don’t give up
on shining,
or bringing men from afar.

www.ingramcontent.com/pod-product-compliance
Lightning Source LLC
LaVergne TN
LVHW040943150826
845672LV00002B/513

* 9 7 8 8 1 1 9 6 5 4 9 2 5 *